MW00488862

DELANEY
STREET
PRESS

Girlfriends Forever

Girlfriends Forever

Great Women Talk about Friendship

by Mary Carlisle Beasley

DELANEY STREET PRESS
Nashville, TN: (800) 256-8584

ISBN 1-58334-064-5

The ideas expressed in this book are not, in all cases, exact quotations, as some have been edited for clarity and brevity. In all cases, the author has attempted to maintain the speaker's original intent. In some cases, material for this book was obtained from secondary sources, primarily print media. While every effort was made to ensure the accuracy of these sources, the accuracy cannot be guaranteed. For additions, deletions, corrections or clarifications in future editions of this text, please write DELANEY STREET PRESS.

Printed in the United States of America
Cover Design by Bart Dawson
Typesetting & Page Layout by Sue Gerdes

1 2 3 4 5 6 7 8 9 10 • 00 01 02 03 04 05 06

ACKNOWLEDGMENTS

The author gratefully acknowledges the helpful support of Angela Beasley Freeman, Dick and Mary Freeman, Mary Susan Freeman, Jim Gallery, and the entire team of professionals at DELANEY STREET PRESS and WALNUT GROVE PRESS.

*For Chandler Beasley
and Courtney Fleming*

Table of Contents

Give me one friend,
just one who meets
the needs of all
my varying moods.

Esther M. Clark

1

A Girlfriend Is...

Friendships between women, especially those formed early in life, extend beyond time and space. Girlfriends may be apart for years, but when reunited, they take up again almost in mid-sentence. Such is the power of genuine friendship.

On the following pages, wise and worldly women examine what it means to make and keep a friend — for a lifetime.

Each friend represents a world in us, a world possibly not born until they arrive, and it is only by this meeting that a new world is born.

Anaïs Nin

The companions of our childhood
always possess a certain power
over our minds.
Mary Wollstonecraft Shelley

There's no friend like someone
who has known you since
you were five.
Anne Stevenson

Friendship takes time.
Agnes Repplier

The most beautiful discovery true friends make is that they can grow separately without growing apart.

Elizabeth Foley

I have learned that to have a good friend is the purest of all God's gifts, for it is a love that has no exchange of payment.

Frances Farmer

The person who
treasures friends
is solid gold.

Marjorie Holmes

A faithful friend is a strong defense;
and she that hath found one hath
found a treasure.
Louisa May Alcott

A friend is one who sees through you
and still enjoys the view.
Wilma Askinas

Friendship is not quick to burn.
May Sarton

Trouble is a sieve through which we
sift our acquaintances. Those too big
to pass through are our friends.
Arlene Francis

The best time to make friends is
before you need them.
Ethel Barrymore

Friendship with oneself is all-important,
because without it one cannot be friends
with anyone else in the world.

Eleanor Roosevelt

What I cannot love, I overlook.
That is friendship.

Anaïs Nin

My friends have made the story of my
life. In a thousand ways they have turned
my limitations into beautiful privileges
and enabled me to walk serene and happy
in the shadow cast by my deprivation.

Helen Keller

One is taught by experience to put
a premium on those few people
who can appreciate you
for what you are.

Gail Godwin

No soul is desolate as long as there is
a human being for whom it can feel
trust and reverence.

George Eliot

My friends are
my estate.
Emily Dickinson

My true friends
have always given me
that supreme proof of
devotion, a spontaneous
aversion to the man
I love.

Colette

2

Sharing

The sharing of ideas forms an essential bond between women of all ages. Without sharing, friendships remain superficial, but once the lines of communication are opened wide, permanent friendships are established.

Anne Morrow Lindbergh noted, "Good communication is as stimulating as black coffee, and just as hard to sleep after." On the pages that follow, thoughtful women praise the value of thought-provoking conversation.

Each person's life
is lived as a series
of conversations.

Deborah Tannen

Intimacies between women often go backwards, beginning in revelations and ending in small talk.

Elizabeth Bowen

To make people into friends,
listen to them for hours at a time.
Rebecca West

If you want to be listened to,
you should put in time listening.
Marge Piercy

Listening, not imitation, may be
the sincerest form of flattery.
Dr. Joyce Brothers

She is a friend.
She gathers the pieces
and gives them back
to me in the
right order.

Toni Morrison

Keep the other person's well-being
    in mind when you feel an attack
    of soul-purging truth coming on.
                                Betty White

The real art of conversation is not only
to say the right thing in the right place
    but to leave unsaid the wrong thing
        at the tempting moment.
                            Dorothy Nevill

If it's very painful for you to criticize
    your friends — you're safe in doing it.
But if you take the slightest pleasure in
it, that's the time to hold your tongue.
                            Alice Duer Miller

It is wise to pour the oil of refined
politeness on the mechanism
of friendship.

Colette

Kind words can be short and easy to
speak, but their echoes are
truly endless.

Mother Teresa

I think one lesson I have learned is
that there is no substitute
for paying attention.

Diane Sawyer

Silences make the real conversations between friends.

Margaret Lee Runbeck

We want people to feel with us more than to act with us.

George Eliot

I always felt that the great high privilege, relief, and comfort of friendship was that one had to explain nothing.

Katherine Mansfield

If one is out of touch with oneself,
then one cannot touch others.

Anne Morrow Lindbergh

Our feelings are our most genuine
paths to knowledge.

Audre Lorde

There's a kind of emotional exploration
you plumb with a friend that you
don't really do with your family.

Bette Midler

The love of our neighbor in all its fullness
simply means being able to say,
"What are you going through?"
Simone Weil

The friend who holds your hand and says
the wrong thing is made of dearer stuff
than the one who stays away.
Barbara Kingsolver

Tears may be dried up, but the heart —
never.
Marguerite de Valois

Laughter is a major defense
    against minor troubles.
                Mignon McLaughlin

We cannot really love anybody
    with whom we never laugh.
                Agnes Repplier

He who laughs, lasts.
                Mary Pettibone Poole

A bore is
a person
not interested
in you.
Mary Pettibone Poole

3

Trust

Without loyalty and trust, genuine friendship is impossible. Edith Piaf writes, "I have always made a distinction between my friends and my confidantes. I enjoy the conversation of the former; from the latter I hide nothing." Mature friendship requires a level of trust that allows for complete candor, as the following quotations will attest.

I can trust my friends.... These people force me to examine myself, and they encourage me to grow.

Cher

A friend can tell you things
you don't want to tell yourself.
Frances Ward Weller

Only friends will tell you the truths
you need to hear to make
your life bearable.
Francine Du Plessix Gray

It is very easy to forgive others
their mistakes; it takes more grit
and gumption to forgive them
for having witnessed your own.
Jessamyn West

There are very few honest friends —
the demand is not particularly great.
Marie von Ebner-Eschenbach

They are most deceived that trust
only in themselves.
Elizabeth I of England

The most exhausting
thing in the world is
to be insincere.

Anne Morrow Lindbergh

Surely we ought to prize those friends
on whose principles and opinions
we may constantly rely.
Hannah Farnham Lee

How desperately we wish to maintain
our trust in those we love!
Sonia Johnson

What loneliness is more lonely
than distrust?
George Eliot

An atmosphere of trust, love,
and humor can nourish extraordinary
human capacity.
Marilyn Ferguson

Without trust, the mind's lot
is a hard one.
Bettina von Arnim

Build a little fence of trust
around today;
Fill the space with loving work,
and therein stay.
Frances Mary Buss

The best proof
of love is
trust.

Dr. Joyce Brothers

4

Happiness

Friends share happiness and help create it. But the ultimate responsibility for a woman's happiness — or lack thereof — belongs not to her friends but to herself alone.

These quotations remind us that while our friends can point the way to happiness, it is our job to live in such a way that contentment is a natural by-product of our thoughts and actions.

Happiness is a matter of one's most
ordinary everyday mode of
consciousness: being busy, and
lively, and unconcerned with self.
Iris Murdoch

If only we'd stop trying to be happy,
we could have a pretty good time.
Edith Wharton

One must never look for happiness:
one meets it by the way....
Isabelle Eberhardt

Cheerfulness, it would appear, is a matter which depends fully as much on the state of things within, as on the state of things without.

Charlotte Brontë

Joy is what happens
to us when we allow
ourselves to recognize
how good things
really are.

Marianne Williamson

Earth's crammed
with heaven.

Elizabeth Barrett Browning

Happy is she to whom, in the
maturer season of life, there remains
one tried and constant friend.
Anna Letitia Barbauld

Happiness to me is enjoying
my friends and family.
Reba McEntire

There is only one happiness in life:
to love and be loved.
George Sand

Happiness is good health
and a bad memory.
Ingrid Bergman

The greater part of happiness or misery
depends on our dispositions
and not our circumstances.
Martha Washington

Keep your face to the sunshine,
and you cannot see the shadows.
Helen Keller

This is happiness:
to be dissolved into
something complete
and great.

Willa Cather

Too many wish
to be happy before
becoming wise.

Suzanne C. Necker

Be happy.
It's one way
of being
wise.

Colette

5

Encouragement

Friendship, at its best, is a partnership in encouragement. Friends encourage friends by sharing hopes, fears, plans, and dreams. When our friends believe in us, we, in turn, find the courage and the strength to believe in ourselves.

Caring women encourage each other and, in doing so, help turn dreams into reality. For a sampling of encouraging words, turn the page.

After the verb "love," the word "help" is the most beautiful verb in the world.

Bertha van Suttner

If you can't help somebody, you ought to get out of her way.

Kate Millet

Seeds of faith are always within us; sometimes it takes a crisis to nourish and encourage their growth.

Susan L. Taylor

But every road is tough to me that has no friend to cheer it.

Elizabeth Shane

It takes a lot of courage
to show your dreams
to someone else.

Erma Bombeck

Before your dreams can come true,
you have to have those dreams.
Dr. Joyce Brothers

God's gifts put man's best dreams
to shame.
Elizabeth Barrett Browning

When you have a dream you've got
to grab it and never let go.
Carol Burnett

Faith is an activity.
It is something that
has to be applied.

Corrie ten Boom

Just don't give up trying to do what you
really want to do. Where there's love
and inspiration, I don't think you
can go wrong.

Ella Fitzgerald

A mediocre idea that generates
enthusiasm will go further than
a great idea that inspires no one.

Mary Kay Ash

Faith can put a candle
in the darkest night.

Margaret Sangster

The goodness, beauty and perfection
of a human being belongs to the one who
knows how to recognize these qualities.

Georgette Leblanc

Dreams pass into the reality of action.
From the action stems the dream again;
and this interdependence produces
the highest form of living.

Anaïs Nin

When we can't dream any longer,
we die.

Emma Goldman

What men and women need is encouragement. Instead of always harping on friends, talk of virtues. Try to pull them out of the rut of bad habits.

Eleanor H. Porter

There is nothing better than the encouragement of a good friend.

Katharine Butler Hathaway

6

Kindness

Kindness is not simply one aspect of friendship; kindness is a prerequisite for friendship. Any girlfriend worthy of the name understands the value of a kind word or a thoughtful act. In this chapter, we explore ways that the well-intended words of friendship are translated into heartwarming deeds.

If you stop to be kind, you must
swerve often from your path.
Mary Webb

You can give without loving,
but you cannot love without giving.
Amy Carmichael

The strongest evidence of love
is sacrifice.
Carolyn Fry

Life is an exciting
business and most
exciting when lived
for other people.

Helen Keller

Accustom yourself continually to make
many acts of love, for they enkindle
and melt the soul.

St. Teresa of Avila

All love that has not friendship
for its base is like a mansion built
upon the sand.

Ella Wheeler Wilcox

What do we live for if not to make life
less difficult for each other?

George Eliot

An effort made for the happiness of others lifts us above ourselves.

Lydia M. Child

Happiness is a by-product of an effort to make someone else happy.

Gretta Brooker Palmer

Sow good services; sweet remembrances
will grow from them.

Madame de Stael

When you cease to make a contribution,
you begin to die.

Eleanor Roosevelt

The entire sum of existence is the magic
of being needed by just one person.

Vi Putnam

We have really no absent friends.
Elizabeth Bowen

True friends are the ones who really
know you but love you anyway.
Edna Buchanan

If I can stop one heart from breaking,
I shall not live in vain.
Emily Dickinson

7

Life

Our girlfriends help teach us about life through their words and actions. If we're wise, we learn as many vicarious lessons as possible before submitting to that most demanding of teachers: experience.

The following observations provide powerful insights into the good life. Girlfriends everywhere are advised to live and to learn, but not necessarily in that order.

Life never becomes a habit to me.
It's always a marvel.
Katherine Mansfield

Life isn't a matter of milestones,
but of moments.
Rose Kennedy

Life is the first gift,
love is the second,
and understanding
the third.

Marge Piercy

Life is either a daring adventure
or nothing.
Helen Keller

Life still remains a
very effective therapist.
Karen Horney

Life itself is the proper binge.
Julia Child

Live with no time out.

Simone de Beauvoir

Fear brings out the worst in everybody.
Maya Angelou

Courage is fear that has
said its prayers.
Dorothy Bernard

You must do the thing you think
you cannot do.
Eleanor Roosevelt

Courage is the price
that life exacts for
granting peace.
The soul that knows it
not, knows no release
from little things.

Amelia Earhart

Do not borrow trouble
by dreading tomorrow.
It is the dark menace
of the future that
makes cowards
of us all.

Dorothy Dix

Pain nourishes courage. You can't be
brave if you've only had wonderful
things happen to you.
Mary Tyler Moore

The best protection any woman
can have is courage.
Elizabeth Cady Stanton

Nothing in life is to be feared.
It is only to be understood.
Marie Curie

Life begets life. Energy creates energy.
It is by spending oneself that one
becomes rich.

Sarah Bernhardt

Faith is the first factor in a life
devoted to service. Without it, nothing
is possible. With it, nothing
is impossible.

Mary McLeod Bethune

Life catches up with us and
teaches us to love and
forgive each other.

Judy Collins

Life, for all its agonies of despair and loss and guilt, is exciting and beautiful.
Rose Macaulay

It is best to learn as we go, not go as we have learned.
Leslie Jeanne Sahler

As long as one keeps searching, the answers come.
Joan Baez

Only I can change my life.
No one can do it for me.
Carol Burnett

Change occurs not just by words or
demonstrations. It is a
question of living your life in a
dramatically different way.
Dorothy Day

Only in growth, reform, and change,
paradoxically enough, is true security
to be found.
Anne Morrow Lindbergh

8

Love

When girlfriends get together, the conversation eventually turns to matters of the heart. And when girlfriends share their own love stories, common themes can be found. On the pages that follow, wise women share lessons they've learned about the heart of the matter: love.

Love yourself first
and everything else falls
into line. You really
have to love yourself
to get anything done
in this world.

Lucille Ball

Let us meet each other with a smile,
for the smile is the beginning of love.
Mother Teresa

Love is, above all, the gift of oneself.
Jean Anouilh

The hardest of all is learning to be a well
of affection, and not a fountain: to show
them that we love them, not when we feel
like it, but when they do.
Nan Fairbrother

Love involves a peculiar unfathomable
combination of understanding
and misunderstanding.
Diane Arbus

A woman who is loved
always has success.
Vicki Baum

When you come right down to it,
the secret of having it all is loving it all.
Dr. Joyce Brothers

Love is like a violin. The music may stop now and then, but the strings remain forever.

June Masters Bacher

Whoever loves
true life will love
true love.

Elizabeth Barrett Browning

Love dies only when growth stops.
Pearl Buck

Ideally, couples need three lives:
one for him, one for her, and one
for them together.
Jacqueline Bisset

Great loves too must be endured.
Coco Chanel

Till it has loved, no man or woman
can become itself.
Emily Dickinson

Love is a multiplication.
Marjory Stoneman Douglas

Nobody has ever measured, not even
poets, how much the heart can hold.
Zelda Fitzgerald

Love is a game that two can play
and both win.

Eva Gabor

Love is the healer, the reconciler,
the inspirer, the creator....

Rosemary Haughton

The giving of love is an education
in itself.

Eleanor Roosevelt

Love itself is bigger than those it
embraces, serves, lifts up,
and transforms.

Rosemary Haughton

The story of a love is not important —
what is important is that one is capable
of love. It is perhaps the only glimpse
we are permitted of eternity.

Helen Hayes

The best and most beautiful things in
the world cannot be seen or even touched.
They must be felt with the heart.

Helen Keller

Love must be learned again and again;
there is no end to it.
Hate needs no instruction.
Katherine Anne Porter

Love doesn't just sit there, like stone;
it has to be made, like bread,
remade all the time, made new.
Ursula K. Le Guin

To love is to receive a glimpse of heaven.
Karen Sunde

We can only learn
to love by loving.

Iris Murdoch

Love will not always linger longest
with those who hold it in
too clenched a fist.
Alice Duer Miller

Where love is, there is faith.
Where there is no trust,
there is no love.
Ellen Royals

Love stretches
your heart and makes
you big inside.

Margaret Walker

Until I truly loved,
I was alone.

Caroline Norton

I think dogs are the most amazing
creatures; they give unconditional love.
For me they are the role model
for being alive.

Gilda Radner

Love conquers all except poverty
and toothaches.

Mae West

When two people love each other, they don't look at each other, they look outward in the same direction.

Ginger Rogers

There is only one
terminal dignity —
love.

Helen Hayes

9

Girlfriends' Advice

Grandma Moses once observed, "Life is what we make it. Always has been. Always will be." In this concluding chapter, we consider a powerful collection of girl-friendly advice for life. Enjoy!

It is very difficult to live among people
you love and hold back
from offering them advice.
Anne Tyler

I give myself sometimes admirable
advice, but I am incapable of taking it.
Lady Mary Wortley Montagu

People are always willing to follow
their own advice when it accords
with their own wishes.
Lady Blessington

As time passes,
we all get better at
blazing a trail through
the thicket of advice.

Margot Bennett

Everything worthwhile, everything of any value, has a price. The price is effort.

Loretta Young

Success is a long climb up
a slippery rope.
Audrey Meadows

I don't know anyone who made it to the
top without hard work. That is the
recipe for success.
Margaret Thatcher

Always aim for achievement
and forget about success.
Helen Hayes

You must train your intuition —
you must trust the small voice inside you
which tells you exactly what to say,
what to decide.

Ingrid Bergman

Trust your hunches...
Hunches are usually based on facts filed
away just below the conscious level.
Warning! Do not confuse your hunches
with wishful thinking.
This is the road to disaster.

Dr. Joyce Brothers

Creativity comes from trust.
Trust your instincts. And never hope
more than you work.

Rita Mae Brown

You have to trust yourself, be what you are, and do what you ought to do the way you should do it. You've got to discover who you are, what you do, and trust it.

Barbara Streisand

No one can make you feel inferior
without your consent.
Eleanor Roosevelt

Until you make peace with who you are,
you'll never be at peace
with what you have.
Doris Mortman

Don't compromise yourself,
you're all you've got.
Janis Joplin

You cannot make yourself feel something you do not feel, but you can make yourself do right in spite of your feelings.

Pearl Buck

Beware of over-great pleasure in being popular or even beloved.

Margaret Fuller

If you're all wrapped up in yourself, you're overdressed.

Kate Halverson

There is a fountain of youth: it is your mind, your talents, the creativity you bring to your life. Tap this source, and you will have truly defeated age.

Sophia Loren

In hatred as in love, we grow like
the thing we brood upon. What we loathe,
we graft into our very soul.

Mary Renault

Trouble is part of your life —
if you don't share it, you don't give
the person who loves you a chance
to love you enough.

Dinah Shore

Treat your friends as you do a picture,
and place them in the best light.

Jennie Jerome Churchill

If you want the rainbow, you've got to put up with a little rain.

Dolly Parton

If you want your place
in the sun, you've got to
put up with a
few blisters.

Abigail Van Buren

If you listen to your conscience, it will serve you as no other friend you'll ever know.

Loretta Young

Time wounds all heels.

Jane Ace

Life doesn't have to be perfect to be wonderful.

Annette Funicello

Sources

Sources

About the Author

Mary Carlisle Beasley is a writer who lives and works in Nashville, Tennessee and is the author of numerous books including several published by DELANEY STREET PRESS.

About
DELANEY STREET PRESS

DELANEY STREET PRESS publishes a series of books designed to inspire and entertain readers of all ages. DELANEY STREET books are distributed by Walnut Grove Press. For more information, please call 1-800-256-8584.